Poetic Ponderings

Booker T. James, Jr.

Poetic Ponderings

Booker T. James, Jr.

Tamika Wells Consulting

Dedication

This book is a special dedication to the female guard who insisted I write a book. She said, "If you do, I'll buy it!"

To all those who pushed me to find an endpoint, and did not let me procrastinate. And to all those who asked me to write, asked me to create for them and to all those who went over my poems and gave me words of encouragement: to all of them, I give thanks. It took everyone to be a ray to be a light and sunshine in this book.

Most importantly, this book is dedicated to whomever will receive it.

To Pastor Emily, Cowboy Nick, my sister Tina, Tamika Wells, for standing by me throughout my ups and downs. Thank you Tamika for taking the time to listen and Claudia for walking me through this process. To Nathan Ross Freeman, Lynn Rhodes,

Tiffany Thompson, Jeremiah "Jazz" Salter, and Leo Rucker because I felt my life coming into alignment with God's words concerning me when I joined Voices from the Dwelling.

I want to deeply thank Steve Doumas and Tiffany Santos, my bosses for the past five years for your committed support. You and the staff are more than family to me. Thank you Brittany from Love Out Loud for always being an ear, no matter what.

To everyone who has taken steps and journeyed with me, in my life, giving words of encouragement and advice; whether I listened or not, I wouldn't be who I am today without it.

To God, especially, who has been teaching me how to separate myself as a mortal man from Him using me as a vessel. I myself can't see myself as a vessel. So, I thank God for seeing me as He sees and not the way I see myself. I pray God continues to use me as a Moses, a Job or a Paul. I pray that He will continue to share words of truth, and send them into the harvest.

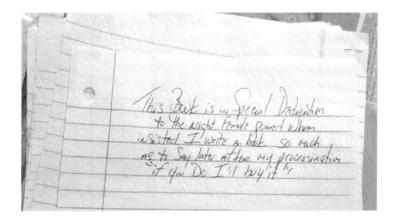

Table of Contents

Introduction......................................pg. 11

Incarceration Inspirations

Beginning Anew: Do You Dare to Dream?
Prologue...pg. 17
Do You Dare to Dream?.......................pg. 19
The Ability to Give Thanks...................pg. 22
Focus on the End...............................pg. 25
Beauty Won't Reveal...........................pg. 30
Let Life Stay a Jungle, You Just Stay a
Lion...pg. 32
The Living Word................................pg. 35
A Picture Painted Perfectly...................pg. 39
Finding the Winner's Life.....................pg. 40
Why Do I Not Smile?..........................pg. 42
Personal Observations of Beauty............pg. 45
Be Best Friends.................................pg. 48
Hidden Verse....................................pg. 52

Real Talk & Realities

Call Him "The Rising Star"....................pg. 57
Wake Up, Man!.................................pg. 59
Who's He? Booker T............................pg. 62
Vibes of 8 South Prologue.....................pg. 65

Vibes of 8 South.................................pg. 66

Jailhouse Hallmark

Happy Birthday, Sis!...............................pg. 73
How Do I Tell Her?................................pg. 75
Happy Mother's Day............................pg. 77
You're My Forever Number One............pg. 79
Pure Heart..pg. 81
Say I Can!...pg. 84
Unfinished..pg. 86
Fly Like an Eagle................................pg. 87
Happy Valentine's Day.......................pg. 90
Thank You, Grandma..........................pg. 92
Simply, I Love You.............................pg. 93
I Love My Black Queen.......................pg. 94
Hey Girl, Happy Birthday....................pg. 96

About the Author...............................pg. 97
About Street Stories from the Dwelling...pg. 99

Introduction

My life has been shaped by chasing after the approval of my father, while carrying the burden of anger from feeling abandoned by him. See, the justice system took me away from my family at eleven years old. I was profiled by a white teacher and wrongfully accused of theft. Though they found the young male I resembled and the stolen goods at his house, I was still forced to go back and forth to court. They never threw out the case. My father couldn't afford to keep leaving work for my court dates or to risk losing my other siblings, so he let the system take me.

That eight months in juvenile "training school" was the most painful experience of my life that sent me on a trajectory of feeling like I always had to fend for myself. No justice, just survival. Since there was no justice, I'd take justice into my own hands. Though I had a wonderful family, mother, sisters and a brother, that season of abandonment, caused me to look for love in all the wrong places.

Rejection made me overextend, overdo things, smother people with my love and push people away. I feel like I've been doing that my whole life. Nothing was ever good enough for my father except for shooting pool because he loved playing,. I never heard him say, "I love you." When he passed away in the early 2000's, I started to see how that lack of approval controlled my life and choices.

To be honest, these poems were written while I was in jail, serving a three-year sentence. I turned myself in and I've spent my years feeling ashamed for all the poor choices I've made in life. Yet God still uses me. He still sees me as His son. I am no longer abandoned. When I truly surrendered my life to the Lord, He justified me when I could never justify myself. I am humbled, and He helps me overcome my struggles daily.

I realized God wasn't like my earthly father. I could never be "good enough" or "bad enough" for God. I live my life in thanksgiving to Him and try not to let offenses, racism and disrespect pile up, but give them to Him. I've made art all my life, but it was a struggle. Once I fully surrendered, His wisdom began to flow to me and through me, my words and my art.

While in jail, my gift of writing, encouragement and drawing still were used. These poems and wisdom were shared to spread the love I rarely received and make people smile. Sharing God's Word, watching lives changed for Him and creating saved my life when I wanted to end it. As I'm going through this writing process, I realize, some of what we're going through is our fear of succeeding, that somehow we will mess it up, which may not happen, but is based on our perception of our past.

It's not unique because everyone has that similarly formulated pattern. But the ones who have become anyone in life, are those who have been able to break that cycle. Putting my gifts and story out there in spite of my faults, is it scary? Heck, yeah, everyday! But the idea of encouraging someone else and being a vessel for God to use, keeps me going. And I try to live a life of full surrender to Him, His will and His ways each day.

Incarceration
Inspirations

Beginning Anew
Do You Dare to Dream? Prologue

This particular poem was inspired by writings from a young lady I enjoyed corresponding with, cellblock to cellblock. I was inspired because this young lady began to write me about wanting to understand more about God. She expressed to me her desire to have a new life. She discovered that her previous self-destruction came from listening to those she called "friends". Yet none of them had contacted or reached out to her in incarceration.

She also expressed her fear of suddenly being all alone and felt she had absolutely no one.

I drew a bird in the card I created for her to help her to know Christ is always with us, even in times we feel all alone. The barren land represents shedding those aspects of ourselves we are trying to release, the trust we have in ourselves and the land we perceive. When we release all to God, He begins to water our land

and give us the true and pure growth we seek in life.

Do You Dare to Dream?

Do you dare to dream?

Can I truly walk away?
Can it all be left behind?
Can I really start today,
Unloading this trash which claims my mind?

There was a time I felt
I needed it all,
yet it all left me behind.
It took this long
23 years for me to see.
Ms. Me...you're just not their kind.

I like to stand upon a hill,
looking out over the horizon.
In a tree, a bird
sits all alone.

I attuned my ear
to listen close
as he hums a merry song.

The sun is shining on valleys below
of green grass and brownish hills.
I feel no wind, the clouds aren't moving,
they're both just standing still.
Everything seems barren
as far as I can see,
Mr. Bird no longer flowing, following his
friends, he stayed here with me.

Everything seemed barren
as far as I could see.
Mr. Bird no longer followed his friends.
He stayed here with me.

The water below
moves along so slow,
its color not blue,
but blue-green.
I pondered again and asked myself,
"What in the world
could this all really mean?"

Beyond the clouds…
there's a beautiful rainbow.
The rumor goes that
at the end, there's gold.
I don't know if this is so,

but if I don't start here, I'll never know.

Finally, I answer my own question
of what in the world
could this all really mean?

A bird alone... a land barren...
flowing water,
color, not blue... but blue-green.

A beautiful rainbow at the end to a goal,
or so the rumor goes.
Encouraging words... that's what it means.
Questioning me...
Ms. Madam,
Do you dare to dream?

The Ability to Give Thanks

You know, I sat down today
and ran reason through my mind,
Seeing how those in the world we live in
are the first to think that they are so kind.

Yet we seem to always find complaint
about one dollar we're not making.
and the one we are told we've earned,
another hand is always taking.

Now, don't get me wrong in what I'm saying.
Yes, the world can be an ugly place,
And our need to be the first to the top
can make the majority, run a terrible race.

We forget, we were awakened this morning,
able to drink a tall glass of water.
The moon and stars went down,
the sun came up,
and God's universe stayed in order.

We pay attention a little bit too much
about the mishaps and daily strife.
And we reject our joy, from day to day
of the constants, in our life.

I may have been one of those people
where negative perception was my best friend,
But I believe all that began to turn
when a woman like you on my journey
stepped in.

Maybe I never expected longevity
of such a friendship to increase,
· But my nights of sorrow, days of drudge,
your presence has caused to cease.

People give away fake diamonds,
at banquets, they serve fake wine.
but I have reason to thank God above,
that in meeting you,
your friendship's genuine.

So now when life's troubles come
and seem daily to knock at my door,
I don't hesitate or feel ashamed
to let my knees hit the floor.

I say, "God, thank You for being up there

and letting me in Your eyes behold."
and as I run down my list of friends,
you're at the top, beaming golden.
So really thank you for befriending me
and trusting me with your care.
There's no more rain, only sunshine,
knowing with my heart, you'll be there.

So I've learned to be grateful.
That I can look upon the sky and see blue.
But I've learned
to be even more grateful
to have comprehended the friendship enclosed
in you.

Some friends give you reason
to look forward to a new day.

Thank you for your friendship, my friend.
Thank you.

Focus on the End

When you sit to write a stranger,
One you have never seen,
If you say "Girl, I really miss you,"
What would that *miss you* really mean?

Would it mean they fill a void,
A place of emptiness in your life?
Or just a kind and friendly gesture,
But not the *missing* of a wife?

How do you say you draw my interest?
I like to know just who you are.
Don't be afraid to draw closer,
You don't have to stand back so far.

She may tell me she has a past,
One she wouldn't want me to see.
But there are things in both our backgrounds,
Things we no longer have to be.

It's very nice when you have someone,
Someone who stops and understands,
You haven't always been the best in life
Of a woman or a man.

The thing about the downtrodden
Of bad people in bad songs,
All they're really honestly seeking
Is caring hands and hearts to lead them home.

There are many who are judgmental
Of what you should've and could've done,
But would the verdict be the same,
If their face was the guilty one?

All wrongs are not incarcerated
Behind jailhouse or prison walls.
Some of life's greatest evils
Are hidden behind those
Who stand real tall.

It may be a name or organization,
A family member or a friend.
It may be someone upheld in public
Which is the gravest of a sin.

It doesn't matter who's to blame,
Someone else or yourself.
Love is when you can turn right
And leave the failures to the left.

Sometimes our eyes are too focused

On the bad things we want to change.
But even if we had been born Mary,
Our failures would probably
Have been the same.

You're sitting there at the red light,
Steady, looking back behind,
Wanting badly to smooth the bumps
You've made,
And all the while missing your "Go" sign.

Now, sure you can lay
And remember yesterday
And listen to what people say.
Or you can know today that
Tomorrow's debt you'll have to pay.

Sometimes our spilled milk
Must stay just where it is
While our new focus
Must be on gripping tighter,
Not as loose as we did as kids.

Yesterday, you couldn't lead the world
Nor sign your name.
Today, you can probably write a book,
Lead the world? Tomorrow that could change.

Always believe you can do better
And reach and walk in that direction.
Stop listening to the naysayers
And give ear to the encouragement section.

You don't have to be like Susan,
Mary, Tamalia, not even Jan.
I don't have to be like that Tony, Robert,
Jim or no other man.

All we have to be is ourselves
And the righteousness we envision.
And when we get up
Out this mud,
Make better choices, better decisions.

I can say you can't make it
And they can say what they want to say.
But it's you, man or woman,
Who makes the truth at the end of the day.

Finally I ask myself
what could this really all mean?

A bird alone...

A beautiful rainbow with
not sure it ends be Gold
But if I don't choose this Change of path,
I'm Sure of one thing.
My true life will never grow

Beauty Won't Reveal

It's not the glow of her outward beauty,
but the radiant inner beauty of her soul.
When it's developed with an integrity,
it's too high glory for others to behold.

A woman of strength sees not herself
but a world around her that's in need.
The poor and lonely, weak and hungry,
a starving people her wisdom can feed.

Her humbleness is in her understanding
that all she has is from God above.
So in all she gives, there is no attachment,
she releases her gift as a dove with love.

Her enemies seem to never understand
how her storehouse is always filled.
Yet it's because every step of her feet
is always in the path of the Father's will.

Although she can walk with her head held
high,
the eyes of her heart are always cast below.
Life's hidden treasures are not to the swift,

but to Lady Wisdom who teaches that our
moves should be slow.

She said, "Let your laughter turn to godly
sorrow,
let your need turn into filled."
Now, when you learn the meanings of these
sayings,
then your life will always be
as though it's all on a hill.

When we separate ourselves from the
equation,
separate our good from our own hand,
then our enemy who was always the spirit of
Satan,
can't conquer us no matter where we stand.

So let nothing of your outward be thought as
your life.
Know the power of your living is your spirit
within.
If you build true love IN your inward beauty,
you will defeat daily this world's evilest sin.

Let your true beauty
be of that...
A mirror can never reveal!

Let Life Stay a Jungle, You Just Stay a Lion

Life can seem like a vicious cycle.
The deepest pain goes round and round.
We strive and pursue happiness,
yet happiness never stays,
it too goes up and down.

It seems to be always us
against the world.
And we are so very tired
of being hurt.
Slowly we tend
to draw in,
believing that
their demon lurks.

We lay on down and close our eyes,
wanting to stay within
the night.
But sure as hell this too will fail,
'cause now,

our own bodies strike.

Could it be that daily stress
slowly taking over our minds,
or is it just pure natural sickness
that comes with living time?

Whatever it is that's always knocking us down
and seems to be winning the fight,
Remember this, it's an old, old drink,
not new, not poured overnight.

Our deepest pain is our question
of God being right or wrong,
or can we understand the purpose
of the weights?
They're only there to make us strong.
Now don't be deceived and believe the lie
that the ground you gain is where you'll
reside.
Yes, that too, someone got wrong!

Life is the dollar made yesterday,
not knowing with it comes sorrow.
See, it'll come less and be all spent.

Leaving, you'll have to make it again
tomorrow!

No matter what you name,
job, family or friends, even loneliness,
it ends the same.
See, though you get it,
you can't keep it,
and therein lies your pain.

Think about the sun
going up and down.
We don't keep it all day long
and we go through life,
day after day,
for therein lies our accepted song.

There's the moon dim, and not the sun,
yet it doesn't bring us pain and sorrow.
We enjoy the lesser light, the dew within,
and the sun?
We believe we will have it again tomorrow.

The Living Word

There's a man I want to talk about.
Oh yes, you know His name.
Though His throne was in Heaven,
To bring life unto you, He came.

They didn't know who He was,
Didn't know He was God's son.
Although they waited on the Messiah,
They didn't know He was the One.

Though He spoke living words,
They fell on carnal ears.
Carnal eyes couldn't see and
Their carnal ears couldn't hear.

He healed their sickened bodies,
Opened blind eyes so they could see,
Brought their dead back to life,
Had them walking on the sea.

He spoke to them from a ship,
Gave them manna and fish to eat,
But when He said, "I'm the Living Word,"
His simple wisdom was too deep.

Today, many want to be like Him.
They want to walk like He walked.
They study the scripture earnestly,
But fail to comprehend with simple talk.

They depend on education
Or the strength in their bones.
Can't they see it's not about them,
But Christ Jesus and Jesus alone?

He told us, "Deny yourself.
Stop claiming glory for what I've done.
How did you win a battle
That on a cross I already won?

"If you could do it, I wouldn't have come
down,
Not from Heaven to Earth to the ground.

"If you could do it,
I needed not come down,
Not from Heaven to the Earth to the ground.
It was me who whipped Satan,
Defending every man, pound for pound.

"I've been fighting to bring you blessings.
It was Me and Gabriel, the archangel,

And to the world, the greatest blessing
Came in a small manger.

"No, your eyes haven't seen.
No, your ears haven't heard.
And your heart's greatest desire
Can't show the manifestation of My Word.

"It's only for you to trust.
It's only good I have for you.
If your stubborn self will only let go,
My Holy Spirit will bring you through.

"People will tell you, 'You need to do this,'
People will tell you, 'You need to do that.'
If I said that you could do it,
Tell them to show you where it's at.

"When I was in the body of flesh,
The miracles were not of Myself.
Even My own disciples,
Waited for power to do, when I left."

"And, behold, I send the promise of my Father
upon you: but tarry ye in the city of Jerusalem,
until ye be endued with power from on high."
                              - Luke 24:49, KJV☐

☐

37

"Not by might, nor by power, but by my spirit, saith the LORD of hosts."

- Zechariah 4:6b, KJV

A Picture Painted Perfectly

I thank God I'm an artist
with the painting, yet lyrics too,
but it would be nice if my greatest painting
would be one depicting you.

Someone's done one of Mother Mary,
one's done of Mona Lisa too.
They've done one of Queen Elizabeth,
but I haven't seen one done of you.

Oh, they may have done your eyes,
your hair, nose and pretty mouth,
but I want mine to paint the hidden story
of just who you are, both in and out.

Finding the Winner's Life

Deep inside ourselves,
There's a fire that truly burns.
There's a destination we seek,
But its way we haven't learned.

Whether young or whether old,
Our end desire is still the same.
There's no difference of the soul.
The difference is how we play the game.

Some try to get there on a bike,
While others take a car.
Some think the way is by the plane,
But even their vision doesn't get far.

Some take off quickly and run real fast.
Then there's those who've
Learned to take it slow.
But one thought they won't ponder
Is how far does this journey go?

We all make mistakes along the way.

A chosen few say that's not so.
But when they close their eyes at night,
An all-alone, reality show.

It's not the world that we battle
Or anything else in our sight.
It's that one thing we can't see,
For it's our own dragons
We must fight.

When you put that dragon under your feet,
Kill him every time, not just twice.
It's then and only then
You'll find the Joy
Of a winner's life.

Why Do I Not Smile?

**(written from the perspective of a
female jail staff member)**

Why do I not smile?

You know, sometimes life
can seem so down.
Not family or friends, cats or dogs
do we want around.

To look outside
and see the sun,
Today, those aren't the things
to bring me fun.

Yes, I'm bowing my head
with my eyes focused low,
'Cause the depression I feel inside
I don't want to show.

What I feel right now
is my normal way.
See, the majority of my life
has seen this day.

The world around me
seems to find reason to laugh.
In keeping it real,
I can't find what's all the hoopla's about.

A friend took my face,
their fingers under my chin.
They said, "Not today, young lady.
today, we're going to win.

"Yesterday, you didn't see
just how pretty you looked
When depression and sadness
you fought and shook.

"I think it's because
when you rose from your bed,
You chose to smile.
The other things you kept out of your head.

"All the people around you
were so sunny and bright,
But it was the radiance you brought
that gave them light.

"So you can make
what you want of your days.
Your ultimate joy

is based on ONLY your ways."

So, for me to you, I encourage you
to laugh, engage and choose to smile.
Live all your days
with the excitement of a child!

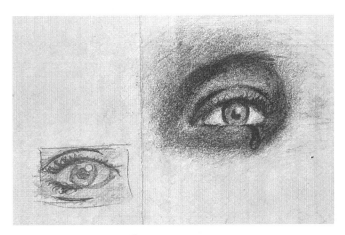

Personal Observations of Beauty

(written for a night nurse at Forsyth County Jail)

I've noticed she's dyed her hair
From yellow blonde to burgundy red,
But it don't matter if it's blue or yellow,
She gives the beauty to what's on her head.

She said if she ever got a tat,
She's going to get one of mine on her!
A tattooed woman?

How many others ways
does she want to captivate my mind?

It's strange I've never asked her
to tell me her name.
For me, I can just call her "Pretty Eyes"
or "Tender Heart", I would love to tame.

She told me she was about to cry
as she stood before me reading her card.
I'm kind of glad she really didn't,
'cause for me not to join her,
now that would've been hard.

Even now, writing this poem,
warm visions of her in my sight,
I smile all over and tell myself,
Yeah, this girl, this girl!
She's all right!

Be Best Friends

I wish I had the ability
To do my life all over again.
I would concentrate only on my inside,
Keeping it pure from wrongdoing and sin.

But then I know that's not possible.
I can't erase my ugly paintings.
So today when I meet beautiful people,
Demons of my past keep the sorrows raining.

Someone said one day
That men don't mature until they're fifty-five.
It's a shame that's a reality.
Not even for myself is that a lie.

I've learned the essence of all of life's gifts
Is to find one soulmate to whom you can
forever bind.
There's no money, nor status, nor material
That can weave your true love
Like the meeting of two minds.

What good is an exotic car
If your soulmate doesn't

Sit in the passenger side?
What good is a house and greatest bed
If when you lay down to rest, there's no
Soulmate next to lie?

If I wrote the greatest poems or books,
The whole world would buy.
If I had no soulmate to share my
Accomplishments,
My spirit and soul still daily would cry.

Some people think having a soulmate
Means having a husband or wife.
But if that's all that it meant,
Then why do married couples
Still take their own lives?

Two can go shopping together,
Both sit on the couch and view the news.
They can twain, create lovely dinners,
But their bedroom pillows
At night sing the blues.

They both can have the top-notch friends,
Jobs that set them up with whatever they need.
But because there's no true spirit connection,
Even the big holes in their hearts will bleed.
The world can listen to their laughter,

Watch their joy on a Coney Island Ferris wheel,
But they both will immediately
Stop and tell you
Without the whole spirit of their soulmate,
These things don't make them live.

I have a question to ask you:
Will being a billionaire
Give you a million friends?
If you were king to every country in the world,
Would it give you true company
That'd never end?

If a man between his legs had a magic wand,
A woman between hers,
Any man she should catch,
Would their spirits stay elevated above Heaven
Now that they can have
The world's abundance of sex?

Someone can give me a yacht,
The highest praise for everything I do,
Live up each night, 500 years,
A different woman,
Still every night laid down,
Lonely and blue.

Has anyone noticed the love of the elderly,

How they can sit all day
Quietly together in a room?
And if one leaves for too long in the kitchen,
The other's soul and spirit is all gloomed?

Their love doesn't need sex.
They don't need the value of a dollar.
They don't need a screaming voice box
When they say, I love you.
It's that silent spirit inside that hollers.

True love can gaze into each other's face
Day-to-day, year-to-year, end-to-end.
Their life gets all of Heaven
And Earth's sunshine.
Knowing right there, right there, right there!
Is my world, one absolute friend!

Marriage is the supreme statement.
It's our crown from where we begin.
But the crumbling down of a marriage castle
When they think they no longer need
To be best friends.

Hidden Verse
Song

Sometimes you think
You're not going to make it.
Life knocks you down and you feel all alone.
But then that's life.
It can be kind or funny.
It's really strange how it plays with our head.
Yesterday there was plenty of money,
Food on the table; all you could eat.
You had a home, you could ll your own.
Clothes on your back, shoes on your feet.
Now today, there's no home.
There's no money, no plan,
No place you can sleep.
Life is easy when you're up on the mountain.
You've got peace of mind
Like you've never known,
But things change
When you're down in the valley.
Don't lose faith.
Choose your cause.
You're never alone.

(Additional verse inspired by a song performed by Lynda Randle called "Life is Easy on the Mountain")

Real Talk & Realities

Call Him "The Rising Star"

There's a brother I've met,
they call him Queasy.
As he's done his beats and voiced his raps,
the flow of his lyrics,
he made seem so easy.

I sat below him
in my own locked cell.
I attuned my ear closely
and said, "What the hell?"

Now normally with today's lyrics,
I don't care nothing for rap.
But as this brother flowed,
he made me want to stand and shout.

Two older brothers expressed to him,
that we thought he was good.
Now moving forward with it,
we don't know, but I still think he should.

I believe tuning his voice
and the right rhythm and beat
will send him flying through doors
and lift him right off his feet.

 I laugh when I think
of his reaction to the words I wrote.
His response, so real,
made his statement really dope.

He said, "Man, I want
a copy of that book.
And my reply shoulda been,
"Yeah, it was done by a *Little Book*."

See, that is a short version
of my real name.
See, Booker and Book,
they're both the same.

So I wrote this poem
just to allow him to see
all the poems I read him,
yeah, yeah, they are written by me,
the one and only,
young old man Booker T.

Wake Up, Man!

As I sit in a lowly cell,
white walls all around,
I can't help but think of what life used to be
when my feet were on the ground.

But then, at one time I was a child,
and my glass of milk hit the floor.
Now there was nothing I could do
but let my feet head to the store.

My mother told me one day,
"Child, take an umbrella with your coat."
I was too foolish even to listen.
Later, I stood there drenched and soaked.

Driving 95 miles along the highway,
not thinking of all it'll cost.
But when I crashed that red Ferrari,
my mind could see the real, true loss.

For sixteen years, that road to school,
later, I saw that one bend.
At the time, I said, "No more.
From now on, I'll follow my other friends."

I wasn't about no diploma.
I wanted to find what made me laugh.
Letting my hair blow in the wind,
And learn what alcohol and drugs were about.

An overdose here, a shooting there.
For those things I didn't care.
Those fools lost, but they couldn't see.
But I saw money everywhere.

You thought the genius was Bill Gates?
Well, this rising genius was on my mind.
You think that's a joke? You imbecile.
Well, stand right here and give me time.

When the sun didn't shine,
Rather darkness came,
I was now seeing
This wasn't a game.

I could no longer go where I wanted to go,
No longer eat what I wanted to eat.
And if these things weren't quite bad enough,
There were nights so loud
I couldn't sleep.

But there was still hope
While doing the time.
I could just stop
And educate my mind.
I could stop taking the road that bends.
And I could stop following those other friends.

When I can see my fault and admit my wrong,
Then I can begin to rewrite my dream.
When I can really care about myself,
I will always add an "I"
In my TEAM.

Who's He? Booker T.

We all have different visions
of what we would like life to be.
Sadly, it's never close
to anything our eyes can see.

The mountains we look upon,
we want ours to stand higher.
And the dollars that one man has,
we want more than any man prior.

They say there was a rich man.
They say he owned an island.
But I want to own the world
and give each pretty girl
her own island.

I want to have an orgasm
like a volcano that'll never stop.
Now the girl who brings that pleasure,
Whoa man, she'll be hot!

I don't want a car
or a truck bound to the earth.
Man, I want a jet
that'll take me to God's forbidden turf!

No, I don't want your jewelry
nor your shining diamond ring.
I don't want your stage of stars
who in truth, can't even sing.

No, I want eyes that when you look in them,
they're amazing to behold.
I want my bones to be stronger than black onyx
and be stronger than choice gold.

I want my heart to have a beat,
the greatest music for your ears.
I want the sound of my voice
to bring your very soul to tears.

I want the glow of my skin
to cause your very eyes to go blind

and the puff of this, my breath,
to be your living lifeline.

I don't care where you search.
I don't care what you see.
You can seek many, many worlds over
and never find another like me!

I know you want to know my name
and what causes me to be.
Well, you'll never know the latter,
but the name is... Booker T.

Vibes of 8 South (the hole)

Prologue

The name of this poem, *Vibes of 8 South*, was inspired by many years spent incarcerated on Vibes of 8 South's solitary confinement lockup floor, away from the general population. For me, with all the diversity of emotion, perceptions and lost identities attributed to that place, expressed mostly in the worst demonic ways, even by the coldness of the guards' hearts and the job necessity, it became a place I literally tried to commit suicide. At times, when there, I begged God to please take my life. For me, being in the hole was like being in a closed dark drum, with someone constantly beating a sledgehammer against it, all while I couldn't see anything.

Vibes of 8 South
(the hole)

Sometimes up on this floor
it can seem there's only you,
as your mind drifts away,
viewing all the things
you've been through.

But the truth is there's others
also locked up here.
At moments, all alone, depressed.
they may feel no one cares.

But then they may just be reflecting
and say, "Just what the hell have I done.
10, 15, 20 days,
man, I can't call or see no one."

Being alone, don't get me wrong,
isn't only despair.
See, the wisdom in some men,
they learn to grow anywhere.

They learn to turn their bad

into victories of good,
raising their heads higher,
realizing their enemies
never thought they would.

The majority of us
were just caught moving too fast,
our heads too high in the clouds,
our feet needing to come
back to the grass.

We miss our loved ones,
and yeah, our boys on the block.
But you know what else is crazy that we miss?
We miss just seeing the damn clock.

Now thinking of roundness,
yeah, well there's that CO's ass.
Well, if you come up here,
you won't see that pass.

No one's into the boys,
so all the men won't do.
So if you are into the sugar stick,
this poem isn't about you!

Every other day is only
when we get to walk.

The days in between,
you only sleep and talk.

If you got your property,
you can read, write or draw.
If you have your clothes, work out
or work out naked, if that's your call.

Some men sit up here
and do some crazy ass things.
And I'll tell you, some aren't faking.
They're really 730 and fucking insane.

You can make friends
and stupid agreements don't cease.
It's amazing how behind locked closed doors,
pussies can become beasts.

But you can find laughter
and life-wisdom building, too.
But what you find on 8 South,
it's a matter of being
all up to you.

If you're seeking advice
In the words of this poem,

Buy you a pair of sneakers,
Write on them, "Jailhouse Shoes,"
Never again to be worn.

Jailhouse
Hallmark

Happy Birthday, Sis!

(for an inmate's sister)

Some say,
"Oh, they know you love them,
So why say it all the time?"
I say,
"I like to assure you
So there's never a question
On your mind."

You're my dear sister
And my heart belongs to you.
And I would never tell you this
If the words I say were not true.

Now you just turned twenty-six,
And yes, I missed your birthday.
But I hope this special card
Will make up for what I didn't say.

You know it's from Big Bro,
And hey girl, you and I,
We are two of a kind.
Now kiss your fingers,

Put 'em to your cheek.
Now that's a kiss from me.
'Cause pretty one,
You're just that sweet.

Happy Birthday Sis!

How Do I Tell Her?

(written for a guard at the Forsyth Detention Center)

How do you write a poem
and keep it polite?
Wish there was no day
and there was only night.

How you wish that person you see very
seldom,
you could see all the time?
Or even when they're not there,
they're still walking through your mind?

Why does life seem funny?
Is there a lesson for it to teach?
For it seems what we want the most
is what we believe is out of our reach.

They say that beauty is on the inside
and not the outer shell.
Well, with this lady, it's both places,
for I'll be damned straight to Hell.

How do I tell her?
It seems she's taken up residence
deep down in my heart.
The love and joy that she brings to me,
I know of no store where it can be bought.

Happy Mother's Day

(written for a fellow inmate's baby mother)

Strange…
these days it seems I can't remember
a day you weren't there,
a time in my life you didn't love me
or show how much you cared.

Oh, I've heard of many fantasies,
never thought that day was true.
Yet while others pay for Disney
baby, I just run straight to you.

You make my heart feel funny,
make my nerves want to collapse.
Now I'm not going to tell you
what happens when you're in my lap.

But today it's about your motherhood
and that special touch you have inside.
There's no concern when it's time for our child
because I don't believe my eyes
have told a lie.

Happy Mother's Day, sweetheart.
Enjoy your day!

You're My Forever Number 1

(created for an inmate to their love)

I can call you my sunshine,
chocolate sundae, or something sweet.
I can call you my little tigress
or my own star I get to keep.

I can call you many things,
even things others can't see.
But I don't care what I call you
in my eyes, you're the world to me!

"Loving you, baby."

But I don't care what I call you in my eyes,
you're all the world to me!

Ah but the thought of missing you
it's like trying to live, without a clock.
or like pain coming into your house,
without even a knock.

Is there really joy in meeting
someone,
who tomorrow, you may never want
to lose.
The type of people, who can't be replaced
and no one, can fill their shoes.

Now many may think, this apply
to a lover,
but then, they just don't understand.
Real love, is not only intimate
because two true friends
can go, hand to hand.

Pure Heart

When I think of a friend,
I used to compare
To a person I can value
And give my best care.

One money can't buy
And material things either
Because their heart is pure
And their genuine love
Is sweeter.

They don't see a need
To fill you with vainglory words
Nor flattering quotes
You've already heard.

They know true friendship
Is keeping it real.
Speaking truth, good or bad,
Is what conquers a deal.

Giving you what you need
Is not always seen
In what they've said,
But they know real love.
Stay focused on your
Road ahead.

They're not afraid
To promote your very best.
Their goal for your life
Is to keep you passing life's test.

They don't treat you
Just in the moment.
Then tomorrow leave you
Hurt and confused.

They're one you know
You can share all of you,
And never ever feel
You've been used.

So I ponder within
Giving to such a friend.

Where do I start?

Of course, they deserve my best.

So I said, I know...

I'll give you them...

My Honey-Dipped Heart!

Say I Can!

(created for a fellow inmate to his daughter)

Did you know that I didn't notice
just how pretty you really are?
How sweet, kind and polite
Your best qualities and beauty by far.

You are coming up in age,
maybe growing a little too fast.
But Daddy's greatest hope
is that your sweetness will always last.

I want you to keep on learning,
fill your head with beautiful things.
Don't be afraid of school lessons.
Instead, take them on to win the game.

Don't let no one say you can't be
the very best in the land.
When a teacher asks for the correct answer,
you be the first to raise your hand.

Baby, learn the meaning of wisdom,

grab knowledge and understand.
And no matter what the challenge,
You say, "I can, I can, I can!!"

Unfinished

(for another inmate)

It wasn't easy, getting there.
And staying takes some work.
But each day of our walk together,
It's your heart I hope not to hurt.

You've been treating me so special,
You've been treating me so kind.
Though life has many ventures,
You're the number one thought on my mind.

I wanted to send you something funny,
Something to make you laugh.
But then I chose to be serious,
To tell you I love you,
Without a doubt.

Fly Like an Eagle

**(created as a big poster for jail's Mental
Health Behavior Unit)**

Am I in charge of my life
or is life in charge of me?
Who gave life permission
to tell me who I can be?

No man goes to war
without first weighing the cost.
If you don't study your opponent,
then already you have lost.

You may think I speak of the world
and just what the world will do,
but your victory in the ring of life
is when you acknowledge
your greatest opponent is you.

My choices knock me down.
My choices in my mind,
the garbage I hold onto,
that garbage makes me blind.

But I can change my tomorrow,
but it starts right here today.
I must change what I tell myself,
stop trying to change what others say.

Yes, Muhammad Ali was a great fighter,
but he won the fight before the ring.
He had his opponent already defeated
before the announcer said, ding, ding.

He never fought against himself.
He never knocked his own self out.
He knew the monsters would
Stand before him,
but said by the third, fourth round,
they'll be out.

He said, "I float like a butterfly."
He said, "I sting like a bee."
If you'll speak better to yourself,
you can fly like an eagle above the trees.

So today, if you'll choose to fight,
knock those dark thoughts
right out of your life.
I'm whispering to you, boys and girls,
I'm screaming to you, husbands and wives.

Dr. Wayne Dyer wrote a book.
It was entitled, *The Sky is the Limit*
if God created you in the heavens above,
why must the sky be your limit?

So fly like an eagle,
high above the trees.
Believe in yourself.
Set your spirit free.

Happy Valentine's Day

(written as a Valentine's Day card to a female guard from Booker)

It's like trying to live without a clock,
or like pain coming into your house
without a knock.

Is there really joy in meeting someone
who tomorrow you may never want to lose?
Many tell you they can be replaced,
yet you feel no one can fill their shoes.

Many will think you speak of a lover,
but then they just don't understand.
See, love can go deeper than just intimate
because even two friends can go hand-in-hand.

We should know without a secret ingredient,
all relationships will surely end.
See, no matter how long
you've known each other,
you still must know how to be friends.

February 14th is coming soon,
and there's special words I'd like to say.
I'm glad I know you this time of year.
I love you, new friend.
Happy Valentine's Day!!!

Thank You, Grandma

(created for a fellow inmate's grandma)

They say material things can be taken.
They don't have to be what you think you see.
But Grandma, the gift you gave to my life,
Not even this world can take it away from me.
You gave me your heart.
You gave me your soul.
You fought for me,
You sweated, even when it was cold.

When you looked into my eyes,
It was my future you were seeing,
Making me always pay attention to my actions,
And my being.
Sometimes I thought you were oh, so tough
And just wouldn't give things a rest.
But Grandma, you knew for this world,
It would take my very best.
So thank you always
For the love that you gave.
I pray you'll see the years
To see the man that you've made.

Simply, I Love You

(created for a fellow inmate for his love)

I could call you sunshine,
my chocolate sundae or something sweet.
I could call you my purring kitten
or my favorite star I get to keep.
I could call you really anything,
even things others will never say,
but baby, words in a poem
can never tell you what you mean to me.
Simply, I love you.

I Love My Black Queen

(created for a fellow inmate for his love)

How can I speak about your blackness
without talking about your soul?
As others can't see past your color,
they miss a heart of gold.

They don't know it's important
for you to give your best.
Because you know the world around you
already put you behind the rest.

It says, *Cast not your pearls before the swine*,
so sometimes it's best
to leave them in the blind.
And while many don't think
you're really that hot,
ah girl, they don't know just what I've got.

Some men don't believe in a precious stone.
They think it's only a fool's dream.

But it was there in the hidden dark.
I found my life's queen.

I love you my black queen!

Hey Girl, Happy Birthday!

(created for a fellow inmate)

It's amazing how it happened
That I met someone like you
Someone so sweet and loving
Someone so real and true.

There's a lot of things in life,
We can give our thanks for,
But my one thanks to God
Is when you walked through my door.

A new birth represents
When we get something new,
And I started to learn to love
When I gave my heart to you.

So for me, as for you,
This is a special day,

And I'll be a fool, if I don't say
Hey Girl… Happy Birthday!

About the Author

Booker T. James Jr. is an American illustrator, author and hymn hummer who enjoys sharing the Word of God and inspiring others to look on the brighter side of life. At the tender age of 66, he still plays basketball, has a mean crossover like Iverson, is a billiards sharp shooter and can be found at festivals creating quick portraits for folks passing by. He took the stage at Voices from the Dwelling to spread his message of justice, community, the Bible and love through spoken word and song. He resides in North Carolina, is a pillar in his community and church, The Dwelling.

Follow Booker at:
www.thedwellingws.org/

Author Booker T. James, Jr.

About Street Stories from the Dwelling

Street Stories from the Dwelling is an answered prayer funded by Wake Divinity School and Gilead Compass. Everyone has a story to tell, testimonies that may help someone else look up and live another day, but it takes vulnerability and support to really put ourselves out there. Street Stories from the Dwelling is the holistic approach to publishing. The program produces powerful storytellers and empowers authors to grow emotionally and economically.

This program cares for the author by offering community and emotional support throughout the publishing process. When a person tells their story or past over and over, they relive the traumatic experiences each time. However, Emotional Freedom Techniques (EFT) and the New Stories somatic healing methods also known as "tapping" sessions are incorporated into the program. Facilitated by a certified EFT practitioner, people are able to get to the root of the trauma to see themselves as victors and not victims. Changing the stories we tell ourselves about our past changes EVERYTHING. When participants in the program fully engage the tapping sessions, it can drastically disrupt the cycles of low self-esteem, self-sabotage, choosing wrong relationships, addictions and even physical pain caused by suppressed emotions. Once a participant learns how to tap, they can self-regulate their emotions anywhere and anytime.

Economically, the goal of the program is to equip each author with their own brand. *Street Stories* is a hybrid between hiring a publisher and self-publishing, which can be extremely costly. Unlike publishing deals, instead of an author receiving 12% or less of the proceeds from their book sales, they receive 100% minus Amazon printing and shipping costs. And unlike the normal self-publishing process, they have a mentor, certified coach, professional editor, marketing specialist and their first box of books and merchandise are FREE! After their first free vending experience at Art Crush in downtown Winston-Salem NC, they have full access to their author accounts on Amazon and can always increase their income by selling their books locally, nationally and globally.

Thank you Gilead COMPASS Faith Coordinating Center School of Divinity- Wake Forest University for accepting me into the LIT Cohort to help bring about this life-changing project! And thank you, Pastor Emily and Deacon Brittany, for supporting this wild adventure to produce well-deserved published authors!

- Tamika Wells,
Published Author and Program Director

They won the victory over him because of the blood of the lamb and the word of their testimony. They didn't love their life so much that they refused to give it up.

☐

-   Revelation 12:11, GW

Made in the USA
Columbia, SC
08 July 2024

38161892R00062